MW01016226

From Where The Trees
Are Standing In The Water

From Where The Trees Are Standing In The Water

poems by
Paddy McCallum

The
Muses'
Company

© 2010, Paddy McCallum

All rights reserved. No part of this book may be reproduced, stored in a retrieval system or transmitted
in any form or by any means without written permission from The Muses' Company, an imprint of
J. Gordon Shillingford Publishing Inc., except for brief excerpts used in critical reviews, for any reason,
by any means, without the permission of the publisher.

The Muses' Company Series Editor: Clarise Foster
Cover art by Doug Biden
Cover design by Terry Gallagher/Doowah Design
Book design by Relish Design
Author photo by Paddy McCallum
Printed and bound in Canada on 100% post-consumer recycled paper.

We acknowledge the financial support of the Manitoba Arts Council,
and The Canada Council for the Arts for our publishing program.

Library and Archives Canada Cataloguing in Publication

McCallum, Paddy
        From where the trees are standing in the water / Paddy McCallum.

Poems.
ISBN 978-1-897289-58-7

        I. Title.

PS8575.C3787F76 2010   C811'.6   C2010-905341-9

J. Gordon Shillingford Publishing
P.O. Box 86, RPO Corydon Avenue, Winnipeg, MB Canada R3M 3S3

In memory of
my father

The fire had power in the water, forgetting his own virtue;
and the water forgat his own quenching nature.

—Wis. 19:18-21

Contents

Part III

Part III

Part I

the music of small animals
leaving my body for yours

Anvil Island

When Al lets a drop of solder fall
into the valve angle-wise and fits
the cap so it sets against any possible
leak of precious fluids, he pulls
his hands away like a god who knows
the world will run without him now
and turns to me and grins and says
"There's a kind of poetry in that"

and I'm not certain where to look
for the wordless poem of action
a friend spoke of following a long fight
with a sockeye near Active Pass,
the boat punching mercilessly against
the ocean's mouth, the fish's body.
Only a god could look upon death
and say there's poetry in that

working so fast there must be
no accident, numbering stars
and sands of the sea, electrons, photons,
the whale at its crest. One god,
a thousand gods, the singular fury
of flesh leaping out of reach until
words in their stalking sequence
clutch gills, scales, the whipping tail.

I play out hooks until the tip strikes
fumble with the plug and dump it
tangled down the wrong black hole
off Anvil Island, where salmon
sleep in a perfect covenant
of day and night. They cast
their sidelong glances at my bait,
then snap it off like blades of light.

The Work Today

Some days it takes forever
to reach the beach
much more of forever
than the day before.

So many steps from the high bank
to this immensity
of round stones
this lumber of the sea.

Each time I return
I am reminded
of some purpose that lies
just beyond the headland

though it refuses me
especially now, when its waters
break foundations
soaking words beneath my feet

The Account

Once there was a book that kept
following me around
though when I turned to look
I found it facing down.

When I held it very near
to the center of a fire
it turned into a paper bird
and expired.

I made love to it once
on a winter's day. Later on
towards evening it confessed
to disappointment.

I tried to befriend it
even offering it my home
and an honoured place
among uncatalogued refuse

and yet when it called
one night in need
I swore I was not in
and did not know where to find me.

If ever I meet it unexpectedly
on the street it spits
and weeps. I
call it rain, keep walking.

Every night its language leaches
into the rivermouth into my
mouth and then from space
like disease upon me.

When I know I'm dying
I write small notes to it
asking for inclusion.
But I know it has taken offense

at my easy desperation.
So I stuff the mailbox with
valentines and sketches.
Leaves settle for my window ledges.

Wild Pigeons At Armour Beach

Three days to Christmas, yet the sun beats
time on a string of wire; some forty pigeons
wild, huddle against arctic air.
Exiled from rafters, they have found
their own affinity.

If they dream they dream of shadows beyond the sea
anticipating songs of arrival.

They have no dreams of family.
No brothers and sisters vanish into the skies
only to return as hawks and badgers.

They have only each other and the long line
that keeps them moving
                                        home today
holding their lives to a bright tree
a ringing in their feet
like the voice of a distant father.

Death Of A Fish

for Emily

We named him for kingdoms of the sun
therefore he caught us - not us him.
Of course there was motion
and his way of smacking thick lips
like Louis XIV. This naming, though
is what we live by and through.

You once named a wood-bug
and it grew. When you named
a wounded chickadee the cat slept
and the bird flew like a prayer
into the boughs of a poplar tree.

We named a trail for the berries we found
and when the town sank a signpost
naming instead for the shape of the land
we kept on naming for what
we took inside. And still do. The names
living on as if we had no part
as if they waited for us to catch them up.

You name the small, the overlooked.
When they swim back into earth
their names still hunt among pebbles
like the sun, like a sunfish.

What Passes For A Field

Some fathers teach you nothing
even when stone upon stone
makes all intentions
clear as rage
these standards still apply
soiling the air
with all that will not budge
an inch or rise to greet
the purpose of a field.

Shovel, pick, prick
up to my ankles
in the hardcore perfection
of home and garden

prying one bruised head loose
from another all of them
are brothers. Each matted
hulk of broken matter
stutters sparks from the edge
of a steel tongue as sharp
as I can bring it down.

The Crossing

At 3 AM the ocean moves
as black as sores around the mouth.

Islands blister in the moon's night-light.
Across the sound a man is pinned
to his bed and will not eat.
The nurses walk like cats
around his plate.

Faces sing at the metal edge,
"Why even bother turning on the lamp?
There is nothing to wait for.
No one is coming back."

Far away from this island of shadows
they're getting bodies
and sex and property.

Tonight in the tide this man is swimming
to the other side without moving

and losing his breath
now refuses even water.

In The Chapel Of The Blessed Virgin

Outside, you were.
Inside, you've become.

Had you never been so large
we would not contain you
blood of the egg
sufficient to the yolk.

When I was a child
I crawled like a child
into a camphor closet.
God was there and you
were there, your breasts
dusty as feet, your hair
a wet cloth drying
too long in darkness.

Now the unintended light
is cruel. The guard
longs for freedom under
an excess of white
but there is only
your cool skin, etched
with lingering remarks.

No one comes in.

Outside in the sun
a billion bodies burn.

Churchgoing

Light through high windows
is something like this
and rain outside, like a dwindling
congregation, the money no longer
flowing in. I noticed today
how cold it is with the heat
turned down and no one
beside me. Only two of us
now and you barely know
I'm here. There used to be
birds in the rafters, but we
gave up feeding them
and their frozen bodies fill
our plates and teacups, later,
after the chanting, when
both of us rise alone.

Coming In

When every thought coughs up
another prayer and daylight
scars the eyes this close to the sea

before the Demerol kicks in
the pain pushes off, smacking a little
but moving steadily west

to harder, dryer reaches of beach
to find your economies of scale
detailing a fear of needles which

though crying out pulls me back again
where numbness is a prayer
of words cut deep into skin

so that we cannot shrink from them
but drink, even breathe them in
and pale stars drift down on rain

to become the fluid in everything,
in the wet sand, in the grating
blood where the prow punches in.

At Charman Mouth

When all the talk is of money
I watch an elderly couple gather
bottles and cans along the waterfront
wiping them into
a plastic bag strong enough
to hold two lives.

They had a boat once and an ocean.
She was good with the knife
and he nosed for fish
like a bear. At dawn
they'd whisper up the mouths
of penniless rivers.

All their talk these days is of money
turning ditch-stones one by
one down a creek bed rich with vital
netting, bones audible
as shells, and surplus wings
to ride the opulent waves.

While Reading Poems on the Bus
I Dream of Emily Dickinson at the Wheel

You riders, she says, will have to wait
this poem can't leave
for an hour or two. Meanwhile
try to remain in your seats, lest the action
cause you to stumble
and miss the sights. To ease our passage
I have covered the walls
with images of wagons, buses,
starships, the blurred wings
of angels, the breath
of distant gods. Outside
the world is rushing backwards
into the origins
of every word, the transit
of our urges into laughter,
outrage, our first screams
as we forsake these bodies
and swerve into the light.

The Jar

I took an ordinary jar of clay
that once held herbs of the rare
European variety, a cork-stopped
squat and reddish-brown jar
of the dried-blood type. I took it
not for size or scent, I took it
for the mouth it had, large enough
to swallow clothes, tears, seasons,
the music of small animals
leaving my body for yours.
I filled it with a closet, rooms,
a city, the road from one
mountain range to the sea beyond.
You'll be happy to know the coast-
line is there along a scattering
of islands, parched sand
that won't leave the skin
no matter how strong the wind.
(I put some in so your skin
will have things to do.)

Mouth to mouth I passed on
eternity. I entered time
and space and the world to come.
Forbidden words, even proper nouns
I crammed them in with stories
from a past that wouldn't fit
no matter when it lived, if indeed
it lived outside the jar I found for it.
I packed each lie, and lying
left my tongue to seal the rim.

Jars are for burying. Who'd drain
a jar of its universe?
I walked to a field, the very center
and cut away the heavy turf
and made a fitting hole. The field
was level, well-fenced, immense,
strong enough to hold a jar this tense.
A good field, where the air
whispers snow. I kicked some soil

back in, and hurried for the gate.

Part II

down a trail only you would follow

Hole

From this day forward
I refute completion:

all the possibilities inherent
in any given moment — this
is where the tongue goes and this
is what the hands do

the number of friends you provide
whose voices I never hear

like unopened mail, trash, drafts
this hole is elective, a surgery
of all that surrounds us, leaving
your detailed single-iris
literate for a time, at any rate
clearly purposed
and clear as to the plan

we have all this right up to the edge
touch it and see if you agree

I Found You

At first, just fingers, then a hand
clutching a piece of bloody cloth.

You told me nothing of yourself.
I waited.

I waited for the pixels
to unravel matching parts.

Such work is dull
and flesh a handicap.

The technology of your body
takes all my intelligence
the display of your mystery
the better part of patience.

Still, my way is best.

Let others praise the freedom of space.
I found you first in a small kiosk
with death in your eyes, the women
tending what was left of your skin
preparing you for memory.

Autoerotic

Even here, where nothing happens
at least I can speak to you.
There is so little time
and the body so few positions
from which to uncurl
and rise and greet the day.

Once on the Web I found a picture
of a man sucking himself.
His hair was damp and his
eyes were closed. He was a forked
labium with a mouth
full of scales. He was a body
on a temple polished
for the light. He was a woman
tasting herself for me
saying, "This is what I mean."

I wanted to reach
through the firewall
and pull him gently
from his mouth
unfold his body

and listen to his story.
(Wake him up?) It was too late.
I had been walking all morning
where the river curves so hard
it almost touches itself
through the tall grass
and the dew and I already knew
what I would find

another small circle
for the tongue
another burnt offering.

The Consolation of the Book

Your text unfolds, depicting
only its blank interior.
There, curled upon each bed of white
lie the innocent with their dreams
in dark ink, the freedom
of type each description
hides. When I open what remains
and press to my face your warm
omissions, I read the way
I have always read you: backwards
scanning the ages.

Mastery

When Peter snaps a lock on the door
and complains that his dead wife
is rummaging through the house again

leaving him notes that resemble
the yellowed skins of poems, the ones
he wanted until they wanted him

we step into the Calgary twilight
surprised to find so many others
walking and talking about the dead

all dead inside us hunched over sinks
and toilets urging us to give it up
and never quite resisting the nightshift.

Your elegy is the first poem I write
each day, until the end, beyond
acceptable limits, the unusual beauty

of you suddenly bald, the chemical
spew in the hall, a radiance of bloody
kisses crying *shut the door.*

The Consolation of Boehme

I gazed into the mirror-snow, God's
thoughts, shaped transsexual.
You are the visitation we deserve.
The white down of the multitude
is constantly falling. At dawn
our world is your frigid
instrument until the rain huddles
us to pulp and the smell
of burnt candles.
It cannot be otherwise, or
the world stands still (just stand
still a moment!)
and muffled footsteps
like the closing of a million mouths.

Conjunction

Living here for a moment
without you (for you seem
a presence, godlike)
without your joining
action, taking forever
to put the nozzle
into the hose I worried
about "into" for
a little too long, then
described each garden
item singularly, the way
those ancient Jews
were wise enough
to pluck out consonants
rounding off the mystery
where it should be
on the tongue, knowing
that to name a thing
is in some way to shame it
setting it beside this
outcome, parting one
to illuminate another
bringing the sun
to this flower, not
two of them, not
a word between them.

Easter in the Woods

Fully present because you are constantly repeated
a copy for which there is no original,
cited anew as code and style
you suspend across these definitions
never accomplished in spite of your cry.

I was waiting in the woods in all positions
each down a trail only you would follow.
I wanted you to see me in my lowest version
a starting point, our beginning again
for you this mobile of marks and voices.

Impossible to form some natural body
a footing free from the risk of force.
There are no previous chapters, no versions
visible from clearing or hill, each trail
entails us to approach this center

with forms of its subject alive in ourselves.
It doesn't matter if you look at me
or take into your mouth the word itself
to gather and split and reproduce.
Let us start here, and never move.

The Consolation of Rain

This is what your light creates
when it trembles with vapors
that evade completion

(when you cannot see a mountain
sometimes for days on end
and know that it is there
that is not completion)

it is for walking on the beach
when the sea is shrunken
taking for comfort
these multitudes, settled
or about to flee

and feathers the size
of small islands fall
in banks of downpour
and I am restless
for the world inside

yet would keep you there
all of you, up there
even if you are transit
of nothing more
than the passing of wings.

Preferences

It has been our privilege
  to push torn messages
through this opening
  the work so dangerous

the space so small
  almost a hole
and the parts which come
  alive can be mistaken

for the flesh of it, not
  the width but the depth
all the darkness it will take
  to fill it, gently

for the hole is a liar
  with a wet mouth
where cutting words
  heal first, then fester.

When I said to you
  look, this is a poem
a finger came through
  and moved on you, as if

it were your own, as if
  it were writing "finger" in
to your mouth: Was that
  your tongue? Yes, I lied.

It Is Outside

Not long after the first —
in a few short minutes perhaps
you would have expected
in keeping with every precedent
out of respect for tradition
a great outpouring

but all that came was silence
oh yes a few chairs moved in the room
many stories were told
and now and then a car would pass
on the street oblivious
someone would shout

not loud enough to be distinct
you could not say for sure
if the voice was male or female
carrying up the white stairwell
the contents of another room
the shoes of the recipient

those who climb the uncarpeted
steps in their stocking feet
with mail for occupant,
a lover, trailing magnificent
pizza scent into the night
chanting addresses, numbers

expecting far too much
even now you weep and shake
believing it has left you
clear about all these preferences
thunderbolt, raincloud, beast –
friend, it is outside.

Part III

I wipe away with dust and grime
the evidence that you precede me

Whatever Is Said Of God And Creatures

in an imperfect manner
in the intellect of the thing
in the agent simply

1.

I'm writing from a place you've never seen
and it's not enough to say it lies
beneath your feet or inhabits the air
like a world of insects, for although
it has motion it does not fly or crawl
but moves instead by consequence
the way angels propel the will of God
or Aquinas calls on angels to write
"The Names of God" by candlelight
and moths arrive from the place never seen
to the periphery of all his thought,
blind spectators to a flaming burst
who write the air like a child's torch
cheering the language of his dream,
clearly an instant; instantly redeemed.

2.

I stood once in a blue room
and placed my hand upon the glass
trying desperately to attract
the smooth white shapes that floated there
in midcourse, always. They looked once
or so I thought, but no act of will
could break the glass or bring them near.
They spoke from a world I'd never seen
and it was not enough to say
they swam or drifted, each
in its own time, beyond my reach.
It would only be enough to go there.

And so it was that on the way upstairs
alone upon the cold concrete
where the stairs turn at the landing
into a right of passage either way
I met a man coming down or up
rumpled but divine, bespectacled,
with hair shooting everywhere wildly
and stooped by the weight of charts
and maps, some drawn in circles delineating
creation to death, the harrowing of Hell,
others plotting journeys from Eden
down to Purgatory and the sea.

"Hold these," he said, "and listen carefully.
Three days and nights I've waited here
'where peaceful silence enwraps all things';
these appearances, well, they come and go.
We enter the world as incarnation,
conquer death, visit Hell, die on the cross
and make our way through limbo
clutching at friends along the way
then reappear for the Ascension -
at that point, I believe, it starts again."

With this he took out chalk and drew
a line across the wall, horizontally,
"Now this is up or down, whatever you please,
the point is, you're standing here,
feet on the line, pulled this way and that,
and the only way I've read about
to break the cycle (though incomplete)
is to speak the name of love and mean it.
Solid then becomes liquid, water from rock.
Here, it's all on my chart."

3.
I stumbled the stairs, one way or another,
back to the room and the blue wall.
I stripped and lay upon the glass
warmer now, and soupy like a stomach.
From all around came the sounds
of their bodies' emergent calls.

The shapes approached cautiously
and with their mouths examined this
and that, pulling, nipping, kissing the way
some lovers bite. Bit by bit
they hauled me through and spat me out
and it is not enough to say I was
in motion, neither floating nor in flight, no
not the tide coming out, not in.
Whatever is said of God and creatures
falls short, as sunlight divides
when it touches the sea,
breaks sublunary, perfect into tears.

I draw maps now in blue details
and charts that move in all directions
up and down, whatever you choose.
My eyes are small to read the darkness.
My mouth exhales the cries of angels
mute, until they breach the burning surface.

Absences

They gave the incommunicable name
to wood and stone...
    —Wis. 14: 21

1.
If I'm to find you I must go out among
remains and take my place with those
who profit best through your neglect.
There, beside a river of blood where
the current turns back at the bend
the bear tears branches every Spring
and strong evidence of you is sought
in yellowed stones and berried scat.
I will look, and it will not be enough.

For you have gone, my companion
of the woods, down where the body bends
like a movement of animals
to the first principle: let us drink
here, alight among these wetlands
before the night can blind us. Here
in lines redrawn from memory
I wipe away with dust and grime
the evidence that you precede me.

2.

Properly, and through likeness you
are predicate; nothing here
begins to describe you and yet each day
we describe you and the paths across your face
that each of us follows to find you
and stick a shovel in the ground
crying "Here, ancestral force,
benefactor, beloved dog or
shape of water underground."
But you're not here.

Gone, who carried our century
into Pacific tides crying, "We'll not drown!"
and drove Qu'Appelle so long
your arm blistered from the window down.

We carry from Babel this hopeless task:
damaged discourse in the wilderness
and speak each name as it regresses
into a cow's udder, into fame,
into sub-artesian nectar.

Gone, who in devastation of the flood
they could not restart. All they had
they poured into your mouth
but, as you predicted, the waters fell
and ran complex as an open sore
and the beautiful ones they hung
from fences or tossed into flames, to live
as those without you live, burning
between the naming and the name.

This River Is A Place Called Home

This river is a place called home
and carves into its lineage
high bank or low
enclaves of mud and sacking set
for the fishing or becoming
of fish. I took my swollen body
splayed it on a stone
beneath the raining progeny
and the river swelled
like the bodies of boys swell
in the leech-warm shallows
textured like skin. This river
is a place called home
where everything in time
lies down, overgrown.
I dipped my swollen hands
and small fish came
for the white flakes dissolving, came
illumined, afraid to feed
too long, or flee.

Traveling Through Bodies

Do we possess language
for this aggregate of colors
this passing through another
into original histories; along
the sudden pull of muscle
do you detect intricacies of diet
and plant life, pre-horse, pre-
contact, recovered here and now
by this one touch as distinct
from another? Why yours?
I wanted to ask, but you had rolled
in sweetgrass. So much

for the dead. Can we engage
even their nominal skins?
I put a girl between my teeth,
Jamaican, exactly as you say
and what came in was not the sea
and salty wind of Kingston, not
(grasping them) tobacco, coffee
but a subtler music, less rhythmic
moved us then in a place less free
as brackish water silts the mouth

over all things that mingle making
a new country, there to feed
ferocious on each other, careless
of culture, myth or legend
drifting apart like wet continents
writing with our tongues a new
relation - moment to memory.

Poetry & Abstract Thought

I apologize for having chosen my examples
from my own little story; but I could hardly
have taken them elsewhere.

   —*Paul Valéry*

That certain word — perfectly clear when you
say it near me, caught in the rush
of your eternal sentence, faithful as long
as your remarks (when you withdraw) halt
time in its flight — that common word
offers a queer resistance.

Well, I've done with life and all of Paris
and all those words that leap a chasm of thought
strolling by without stopping, dancing
on planks along the Demimonde Bridge
where words themselves in their rush
to outdo each other form and dissolve.

Look at yourself. What is that piece of paper
in your hands demanding that I forget
your nature? Dirty. Dirty little paper-trail
of words for *mouth* — the same dozen words
getting away with it and skipping off
while we try to think of what dictionary to use.
The moment I pull you down another street
and remove your temporary function
you become the terrible end of desire,
monkey-noise of *sir* and *choke* and *please*.

I ask you for a light, and you give me a light.
I lead you down the street by a chain
of fragments acting like the real thing
gripped by a rhythm outside myself
murmuring, I am not this person. I cannot
sing. Your beauty is an error of transversion
the cunning organization of your body
walking between my steps and thoughts
a few lines from now; many thereafter.

You know I'm borrowed language. Hired
by the hour. Nothing pure. A coupling
of sound and sense like a dog at a hole
something like a spell of broken glass, crack-
talk, the money changing hands for a genuine
response, a unity of music permitted
for a moment to act upon us, a maid at work
without apparent effort, singing on her knees
to the logic of the cries next door.

Empire

The great society of the alley
has found its way home
carrying ample treasures
one by one
offerings, sustenance, a little
something tucked away
for the children
                          it goes on all day
each morsel trucked
below the dusty lane.

I watched one bloody seed
of raspberry elevate
a culture, a single blade
of grass unfold new
testaments of earth
the progress vulnerable
to heat, the plow, the great
wheel's scorn

                              and went in
converted warehouse tubing
tending down, each face
averted, not a crumb
out of place. I pulled
my weight as good
as anyone afraid
of the rumble upstairs
the 4 by 4s and boot-crunch
the fenceposts cutting in
and putting no little
strain upon the retrofitted
buttresses
                    pushing back
to preserve the family
hoards of fuel for
the slave-trade, the new
expansion, dreams
of a way through a solid-
looking edifice of cloud
mountains, tribal
gods beyond number
digging infinite portals.

Standard Operating Procedures

After three days we turned the sound down
and read only lips
the smoke curling dense languages
each soul a dirt corpuscle
each name calcified to
new stones, new fists.

As I stood in a freezer the size of the moon
I looked up
into pallets of food all the way to heaven
letting go as I did
of all my forms
and the building shook and pieces
of lives yet to be lived
thawed blood-red around me.

I looked up past the downrush of steam
to see the trucks waiting
hearing nothing of their former growl
the forklifts idle
and more distant still
the frenzy of demand
no delivery could fulfill.

So, after three days with the sound down
I looked out
the immense walls of the warehouse broken open now
the product exposed
no trucks at Gate Four
the guard directing storm petrels
come down, come down.

After three more days with the picture off
my work resumed
gathering netfulls of fish for the flash-freezing
collating pallets of ice
while trucks came and trucks flew
into perpetual dawn

driving for days with the music turned on
watching horizons burn
recomposing neglected songs
presuming some difference in the world
or the land, silence
in the mouth like dust or bone.

Part IV

to think of you, stopping here

From Where The Trees
Are Standing In The Water

*Place names form a permanent register or index of the
events or course of a country's history; they are fossils
exposed in the cross section of that history, marking its
successive periods; and so lasting are they that records
in stone or brass are not to be compared to them.*

   —*William Francis Ganong,*
   A Monograph on the Place Nomenclature
   of the Province of New Brunswick, 1896

***all language simply the knowledge of naming
simply all it has become***

   —*bp Nichol, Journal*

"Where are you from?"
this man was asked.

"From where the trees are standing in the water
and I'm looking for a home."

"Then," said the questioner, "settle here,
and that shall be
the name of your village."

1.
Listen.
            A thundering noise.
Geese? The surf? A river
bending around its own
back bending below
the big branch

from the saincte croix
to the barred harbour

a river of the long tideway
(good for everything)

2.
From the cove of the jellyfish
on the back arm

from the saint of the wilderness
in the land of cod

among stands of birch
and their broken roots

beyond the Passamaquoddy
where the Bear tears branches

through broken marsh
to the House of God

from good canoeing
down the extra 'S'

for the Sun King
on the imposing mound

out of Terre des Bretons
by scurvy and the Queen

beyond the German guns
past the split cape

from women at the falls
and the falling unto death

across the marsh impassable
these rivers separate

3.
Out of the egg
the five-year larvae

out of Sikusi
the unfrozen and free

out of archean gneiss
shards of aurora

out of the ice bird
feathered limestone

out of corn and the sea
là où c'est fermé

out of eshko-timiou
the end of deep water

out of the neck
the white snake foaming

out of three arms
the ironmaster's breath

out of vapour
forks of Magog

out of famine
the unmarked grave

4.
Into the white ship
le chemin qui marche

into the white ship
the trees that cure

into the white ship
the rio de San Roque

into the white ship
ashes of Gold Mountain

5.
From the place where there are houses
to the place of the bowhead whale

this man hopes of passage
'lesse evry day'

he is a white ship adrift
on an inland sea

something gained
in the distance, something lost
in the navigation

6.
Out of Matonabbee
a lump of ore

around stones in the sea
two caribou

deep in the money place
copper knives

down the River Disappointment
a discoverer

from Inuvialuktun
this place of man

7.
There was this white ship, a man
trading for otter

this white ship with a thousand
worms in his belly

he sailed on a raindrop
through ghostland

he walked like a clerk

they say he was
a king once
crying for his lover

8.
Within one river
another: tacoutche

into de fuca's sea
Phokas, west of Athens
inside nanymo
the great and mighty
in nootk sitl
waters surround mountains
down Kwikhpak
the river's great throat

into ontare
the copper cliffs

within Manitou
a dwelling place

9.
Out of the falls
the Blessed Virgin

on the Sleeping Giant
a lakehead

out of radiocarbon
fish weirs, a line

along the spirit strait
a talking beach

from lac des prairies
a river of blood

in the manoteusibi
a stranger's stream

around the whale's mouth
trichinosis, ivory

beneath the sunless city
gold in the hole

in the great hall of heaven
paradise

10.
From where the reeds
are in the mouth
to the buffalo narrows

reeds of peace
reeds for the slave

reeds to slow the white ship

(Look, the boats turn about
in the water
like broken reeds!)

11.
Into the hammer water
stakes for the salmon heart

into the whitefish
transit of tongue

into the rapids
white hooves and fossils

into the big river
sparks and floodland

into the walking crow
smoke of burnt lodges

into the clay bank
the fort, abandoned

12.
Across a meadow-portage
to the English camp

past montagnes des cyprès
on the long march

out of Banbha
to the valley of ten peaks

past caladh a gharaidh
to the clear running stream

over stoney brook
to the place of flowers

through murky waters
to boomtime

13.
Beyond mistahay-muskotoyew
la grande prairie
is a deep-basin gas field
for sowing grain

she is waiting
surrounded by apples
alive outside
the exploding train

camels and peacocks run
from the quilt
where her Lord walks
into soft stone

14.
Onto vilni zemli
the sheepskin coats

onto the woodland
two hundred fifty dollars

onto the free land
the bunkhouse boys

onto the first train
marquess
princess
regina

onto the bay farm
a haven by the wall

15.
In this occasional lifetime
in the middle of our triumph
(named by some as augury)
wagons approach, open their decks
and throw cargo on the beach

It is an endless afternoon
of hot lights, tremors overhead
each temporal artifact
an appellation, claiming the act

16.
Over the fields
mountains for the king

in the rank of muskox
a greeting

along the golden snow
caribou crossing

behind the pierced rock
chaloupes in full sail

out of piekouagami
the voice of one crying

in the blood of Lot 15
smallpox and tea

within the gut of the whale
the puckered river

in the sand of the islands
bodies of women

under Deux-Montagnes
ashes of convent

17.
From where the trees are
standing in the water
to the crossing between falls

from perception to pattern
along indices of stone
down the culture of salmon

beyond the Somme
to the white ship bringing
beer and auto parts

sausage makers, distillers,
electrical equipment
each from the other

the loser, the hero
circle in the big lake
spearing fish from the bow

18.
From the rocky trench
long winters

from chin-ch-ago
great waters

from sandstone cliffs
shade-bones

from amakowis
the big house

from amiskwachie
beaver hills

from saamis
the war bonnet floating

from Siding #12
dictionnaire des Cris

from the bull's head
judgement and law

from the red doe blinking
on the south shore

to witaskiwinik
this place of peace

19.
Its name is a fruit with too much wood
where the Cree cut berry willow
for arrow shafts

Its name is a bent bough
for catching fishes
where the river narrows
and water comes fresh

into a cluster of dwellings
a kingdom

this man is not listening
(he has a head full of train tracks
and a pile of bones)

when he wakes up
there is only a branch in his hand

A Dwelling Place

Father, you sow these seeds
in maps so clear the fish can breed,
their ponds perfected first in time
and only then set free of mind
through labour, yes, with faith's
teeth barely held in place,
a summer house and reservoir
to troll your salt-water hooks.

Not ideas anymore, but thoughts
like sequenced cannon overtake
this centre's habitat: the path
through woods de Poutrincourt made
over Gut shoals barren at low tide

above the falling water of the basin
into a drainage ditch; the winter
ate you like a bug eats shit
where you, propheta, drew history
as consummate meadow, goats,
an alphabet of forge and garden
carved through a palisade of stakes.

When I have stopped as you stopped
well past this place as we found it
beyond the rank of oxen, the ashes
of convent, possessed of nothing more or less
than descriptors cut for the bend
in the river, the trees in the water

I will think of you, but not often, my
companion of the woods, for I will be
at bedside with another generation
wholly aware of names receding
under morphine and peach blossoms
desperate to contain each dream each

intention, as we beheld one morning
the sands of islands, the voices of women
and called to them as they fell away
you are the place, supreme and separate
and turned, then, to vellum or deerskin,
scratched our decision, and paddled on

to think of you, stopping here, where
I hurt all over and lose my way to
the ground of things like a compass
dropped in the bay, or a stone marker
split eventually by the word moisture

thinking of you and your perfect fish
on the land you made where birds came
and named not for the coming hither
or going hence, but as dwelling place,
inhabiting this earth, where one turns
eternally to a marker, while another
brushes snow from his name.

Finally

It is always there, next to your skin,
if you look on it that way
Martin Buber

1

a system, a catalogue or register
of all we carry; an expression
accounting for all that is connoted in
all we would say, an offbeat
& wondrous fragment, stepping
between actions with all the force
of a noun, breaking into
waves & furrows, into
dreams, shades & concepts,
an offering, a caution, the last
of the water, our name
for the end of days

2

an emergence, a descent
inhering birth yet odourless,
a redaction of original histories
completing a cycle, having caused
to begin, therefore
beginning, a correlation
of various accounts written
to serve so many purposes
so many feelings, a winning back
of all that was lost, an irony
of the body, an arrival

3
a great expanse, a main area,
the mass of it surrounding
quantities of anything: love,
cement, marshes, flesh, the scent
of its vast movement in
a breeze, the subtle differences
as in did you touch it? see it?
infinite of turning, from the surface
inwards, from the front
to the back, abstruse, of
all colours mostly darkness

4
a crucial map, the unusual
nomenclature of ghosts, a listing
of the properties of rainbow
waterfalls, an exploration or inquiry,
an accord between faith & reason,
a basis for consideration,
a principle of action, of form
heavenly & as to this body
where it stumbles below
the heart, a hindrance

5
the laws & graces, habits
& virtues of non-rational
appetites & the shades of passion
in parrots from Madagascar
& yields of grapes
in meadow-plants of delicate
green bracts of purple-
red blooms beside a small sofa
made for this, to be inclined
there with a mark on the skin
to cherish, with

6
a structure of bones with the flesh
apart, a bulk or majority,
movable in flux issuing streams
of water, objects of angelic
intellect enclosing wine, music,
apparent knowledge, pierced
& burned, concealing weapons,
forming itself in images of
fanciful things, prepositional,
syllogizing while asleep
each flaw, each fetter

7
a general idea without discernible
reality, not further things
or features of things, as in
thinking of Emily Dickinson
& conjuring her, disputing her
knowledge, authority of forms,
recipes, sets of numbers,
physics & phrases, even a sentence
pointing beyond knowledge
like the shape of a river beyond
the bend in that river, the 'she'
in "all that she knew gleamed forth"

8
a door, a window, a hatch leading
into or out of (a room?)
a disputation, a pair of wings,
the legends of those wings,
the paths along the river
leading also to the sky,
the manner of them, the conditions
under which recurring motifs
connote knowledge, the
memory of freedom, an act
of doubt, & departure

9
a portion of space occupying
some natural position, a dwelling
not in us but around us,
a cry from further back beyond
this field, this town, this river
issuing from the will through
points of inquiry, asking
of origin, location, a common
genus, the end of motion,
the realm of the eternal
as unexpected, & tangible

10
a seat of volition, of thoughts
& desires, each of the other,
focused or lost, embracing
remembrance & scolding the past,
its willful bending, both wake
& ocean, a sovereignty of dead
phrases over persistence
of the dead, a light in the hallway
the body naked under it, re-
turning to touch itself, as if
it were located here, within